YOUNG AMERICA

The First Continental Congress

Marylou Morano Kjelle

Mitchell Lane
PUBLISHERS
2001 SW 31st Avenue
Hallandale, FL 33009
www.mitchelllane.com

Mitchell Lane
PUBLISHERS

Printing 1 2 3 4 5 6 7 8

YOUNG AMERICA

The First Continental Congress
The French and Indian War
Life in the Original 13 Colonies
The Second Continental Congress
The Signers of the Declaration of Independence
Stamp Act Congress
The Story of the Declaration of Independence
An Overview of the American Revolution

Library of Congress Cataloging-in-Publication Data
Names: Kjelle, Marylou Morano.
Title: The First Continental Congress / by Marylou Morano Kjelle.
Description: Hallandale, FL : Mitchell Lane Publishers, 2018. | Series: Young America | Includes bibliographical references and index. | Audience: Ages 8-11.
Identifiers: LCCN 2015003202 | ISBN 9781612289779 (library bound)
Subjects: LCSH: United States. Continental Congress—Juvenile literature. | United States—Politics and government—To 1775—Juvenile literature. | United States—History—Revolution, 1775-1783—Causes—Juvenile literature.
Classification: LCC E303 .K55 2018 | DDC 973.3—dc23
LC record available at https://lccn.loc.gov/2015003202

eBook ISBN: 978-1-61228-978-6

CONTENTS

Words in **bold** throughout can be found in the Glossary.

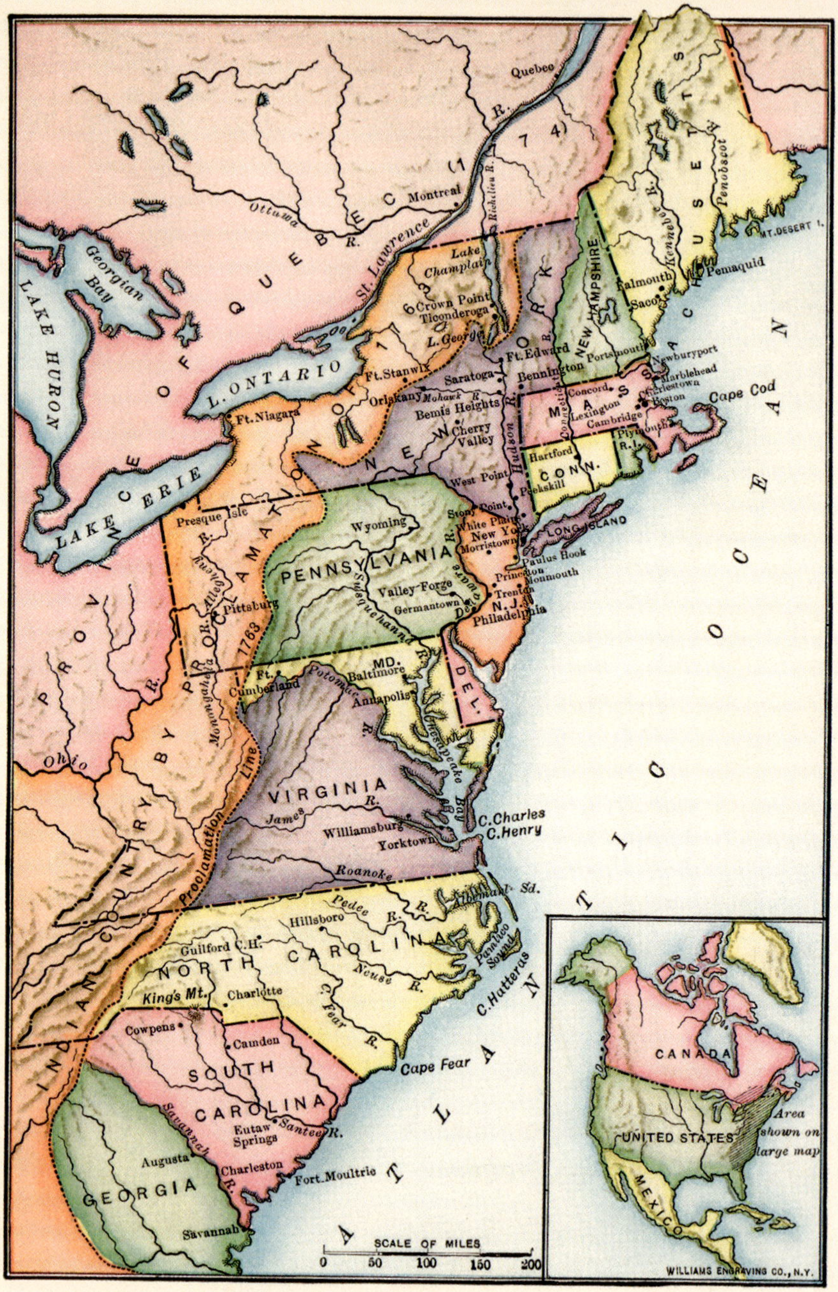

In 1776, the year the Revolutionary War began, the 13 original colonies stretched along the east coast of what is now the United States of America.

1

Gentlemen Meeting Together

On September 5, 1774, delegates from the American colonies gathered in Philadelphia for the First Continental Congress. Some of the men (and in those days only men could be delegates) had traveled for weeks on horseback and by coach over dusty, muddy, and rut-filled roads. Others, arriving in Philadelphia by **brigantine**, had braved choppy seas.

Whether they hailed from the North or the South, or had traveled by land or by sea, every delegate was aware of this significant moment in history. By forming a congress, the colonies were sending a message of unity to their mother country, England, and to their monarch, King George III.

For years the colonies had borne the burden of unfair taxes, harsh laws, and strict British rule. Then, in March 1774, the British Parliament passed the Coercive Acts. These laws, aimed mostly at the Massachusetts Bay Colony and its largest city of Boston, were Parliament's severest so far. The colonists found the Coercive Acts so unbearable that they renamed them the Intolerable Acts.

CHAPTER 1

Trouble in Boston

One of the Coercive Acts, the Boston Port Act, closed Boston's port to commerce and trade. The port closing was Parliament's way of punishing Boston for the Boston Tea Party (See the next chapter for an account of this event). The Act kept the port closed until the colonists repaid the East India Company for its tea that had been thrown into Boston Harbor.

The port was Boston's lifeline to the outside world. The city faced the possibility of starvation without the food and other provisions carried by the ships that docked there.

In the 18th Century, Boston's port was a major gateway for supplies for the Massachusetts Bay Colony, as goods were brought into the city by merchant ships from all over the world. When the British closed the port in March 1774, many Bostonians feared they would starve to death, but help came from some of the other colonies.

Parliament saw closing the port as a way of making an example out of Boston by showing the other 12 colonies that disobedience had serious consequences.

Boston, on the other hand, was **adamant** that it would not pay for the destroyed tea. One of the duties of a royal governor was to keep Parliament and the king up to date about colonial affairs. In late 1774, Pennsylvania governor John Penn wrote that "the general Temper of the People, as well here, as in other Parts of America, is very warm. They look upon the Chastisement of Boston to be purposely vigorous . . . and in short that Boston is Suffering in the Common Cause."[1]

Parliament thought the strict measures of the Coercive Acts would terrify the other colonies. But it was wrong. At great risk to their own safety and liberty, the other colonies supported Boston by sending food and supplies to the city. These worthy gestures were helpful, but they did not address the root of the colonists' problems. It seemed apparent that King George and Parliament no longer viewed the colonists as true Englishmen, and therefore did not respect their rights and liberties. In addition, England was exploiting the colonies' **economy** for its own good.

Many people felt that British rule needed to be confronted. After all, if Parliament could punish Boston by closing its port, which colony might be next to experience Parliament's wrath? And in what way? The time had come for the colonies to stop acting like independent **provinces**. They needed to present a united front. And the first step toward presenting a united front was to call a national congress.

Holding a meeting of all the colonies was not a new idea. Benjamin Franklin had proposed such a meeting in 1773.[2] But at that time, the colonies hadn't been ready to organize into one united body or speak and act as one voice. The idea was just too **radical**.

Growing Support

After the Port Act closed the port of Boston, however, the idea of a national congress began to sound like a good idea. The colonies had already established committees of correspondence as a way to share information. In the spring of 1774, the Massachusetts Committee of Correspondence sent a petition to its 12 sister colonies. The petition asked them to retaliate for the Coercive Acts by closing their ports to British ships. The Committee also requested that the colonies **boycott** British goods.

The New York Committee of Fifty-One was a group made up primarily of merchants. They were afraid of losing business if the ports were closed and British goods were boycotted. The merchants suggested a national congress instead. On May 23, 1774, they wrote, "We conclude that a congress of deputies from the colonies in general is of the utmost moment; that it ought to be assembled without delay, and some unanimous resolution formed in this fatal emergency, not only respecting your deplorable circumstances, but for the security of our common rights."[3]

Soon the colonies of Maryland and Virginia also called for a national congress. Since it would be the first congress of its kind held on the North American continent, it was called the First Continental Congress. The opening day was set, and an **agenda** was planned. The city of Philadelphia was chosen as a meeting place. The largest city in America at the time, Philadelphia was located more or less geographically in the center of the colonies.[4]

Each colony selected delegates to represent it. Some chose delegates by holding special elections. Other delegates were appointed by local legislatures or committees of correspondence. The number of delegates from each colony was based on how many it could afford to send. Some men paid their own way for the privilege of being a delegate. All totaled, 56 delegates attended the First Continental Congress.

A Group with Varied Backgrounds

Who were the men chosen to represent the colonies at the First Continental Congress? For the most part, they included the most powerful, wealthy, and sophisticated men in the colonies.[5] All had been born in one of the 13 colonies. Thirty-two delegates were lawyers, but only half earned their living practicing law. The rest were plantation owners, farmers, merchants, or gentlemen who lived on land and money they had inherited.

Most of the delegates had attended college, and six had studied law in London. A few delegates had only the most basic schooling. One was self-educated.[6] They ranged in age from 24 to 67. Nearly all had served their home colonies in some way. They had been members of the legislature or committees of correspondence. Some were speakers of their colonial assemblies—the highest elected office in their provinces.

Differing as they did in experience, education, and age, the delegates to the First Continental Congress appear to have been an **eclectic** group. Observing the assembly on the first day of the congress, Massachusetts delegate John Adams might have been thinking the same thing. In a letter to his wife Abigail, Adams wrote "Fifty gentlemen meeting together, all strangers, are not acquainted with each other's language, ideas, views, designs. They are, therefore, jealous of each other, fearful, timid, skittish. Yet the congress all proclaims the same political principles!"[7]

George Washington had commanded troops during the French and Indian War (1754-1763). He and seven other men from Virginia served as delegates to the First Continental Congress. At the Second Continental Congress (1775-1781), Washington was named commander-in-chief of the Continental Army.

2

The Road to Philadelphia

The events that led to the First Continental Congress had begun more than 20 years earlier. From 1754 to 1763, Great Britain had been at war **simultaneously** with several European powers. In Europe and India, the conflict was known as the Seven Years War. In North America, it was called the French and Indian War. It began when the British and French fought for control of the Ohio Valley, which lies between the Ohio and Mississippi Rivers, and spreads northward into Canada. Great Britain was victorious in the French and Indian War.

These wars were costly to fight. They nearly caused Great Britain to become **bankrupt**. Afterward, many British troops remained in the colonies as protection from hostile Native Americans. England believed that the colonies should help pay for this protection. They decided that placing a duty, or tax, on an imported product was the best way of raising the necessary money.

In April 1764, Parliament passed the Sugar Act. This act taxed the molasses that the colonies imported from countries that were not part of the British Empire. The colonies used molasses to make rum. So one immediate result of the Sugar Act was a decrease in the colonial rum industry, a major source of income. The Act also reduced the number of foreign markets where the colonies could export their goods. This resulted in a decrease in colonial sea trade.

"No Taxation Without Representation!"

The **political** consequences of the Sugar Act were even more important than the economic ones. According to British law, citizens could be taxed only if their elected representatives agreed to the taxation. The colonists were not represented in Parliament. Therefore, they maintained that Parliament could not tax them. The slogan "No taxation without representation!" became a rallying cry throughout the colonies.

Colonial newspapers encouraged protests of the Sugar Act. On May 31, 1764, a letter was published in *The Boston News-Letter and New-England Chronicle.* Although it is not certain, this letter is thought to have been written by Sam Adams, the leader of a Boston protest group called the Sons of Liberty. In part, it read, "But what still heightens our apprehensions is that [the Sugar Act] may [lead] to new taxations upon us: For if our trade may be taxed, why not our lands? Why not the produce of our lands and everything we possess or make use of?"[1] The letter voiced what many colonists were thinking. What item would Parliament tax next?

The colonists sent letters protesting the Sugar Act to Parliament, warning that Americans would boycott English goods if the Act was not repealed. Many newspapers supported a boycott. An article in the *Pennsylvania Journal* on August 23, 1764 urged American women to stop wearing the fancy dresses that came from Europe. Instead, the arti-

Colonists expressed their anger over Britain's passing of the Intolerable Acts by targeting members of the customs commission. Customs commissioners were responsible for seeing that taxes were paid on goods coming into the port. Colonists punished customs commissioners by pouring hot tar over them and then covering their bodies with feathers. This commissioner of customs, John Malcolm, was also forced to drink tea.

cle said, they should wear "decent plain Dresses made in their own Country."[2]

One Tax Replaces Another

The boycotts were successful. They hurt Great Britain's economy and the Sugar Act was repealed in 1766. Only a year before, however, Parliament had passed the Stamp Act. This act taxed all printed material, including newspapers, deeds, wills, advertisements, contracts, even playing cards. Each of these materials required an official seal to prove that the tax had been paid.

Once again the colonists protested. But for the first time, colonial leaders began to understand that they had a better chance of standing up to Parliament if they presented a united front. In October 1765, the Massachusetts House of Representatives invited all the colonies to attend a Stamp Act Congress. The purpose of the congress was to allow the colonies "to consider . . . a general and united, dutiful, loyal and humble representation of their condition to His Majesty and the Parliament; and to implore relief."[3]

Nine colonies attended the Stamp Act Congress, held in New York City. The royal governors of New Hampshire, Virginia, North Carolina, and Georgia refused to let delegates from their states attend. On October 19, 1765, the Stamp Act Congress passed a Declaration of Rights and **Grievances**, as well as addresses to both King George and Parliament. While maintaining loyalty to the king, the Declaration clearly stated that taxing the American colonies without their consent was unconstitutional. Taxation also violated their rights as Englishmen. "[T]he only representatives of the people of these colonies are persons chosen therein, by themselves; and . . . no taxes ever have been or can be constitutionally imposed on them but by their respective legislatures,"[4] the Declaration read.

The Colonies Come Together

The Stamp Act Congress played an important role in uniting the colonies. It also marked the first time that representatives from several colonies came together. The colonists discussed their grievances and shared ideas. To be sure, the delegates had conflicting opinions. But for the first time, the colonies realized that they also had a lot in common. When the Stamp Act was repealed in 1766, the colonies also realized that they could have an impact by acting together.

A political cartoon can be used to make a point about an issue. Cartoons like this one appeared in newspapers after the Stamp Act was repealed. It shows wealthy Englishmen attending a funeral for the Stamp Act. These Englishmen mourned the repeal of the Stamp Act because they had profited from it.

These realizations would be put to good use when Parliament passed the Townshend Acts in 1767. This round of taxes targeted products the colonists imported from England, such as glass, paper, and tea. By this time, Parliament had also put into place harsh penalties for trade violations, such as the **smuggling** of taxable items into the colonies. Some of these penalties included seizure of ships and cargoes. Once again the colonists retaliated by boycotting British imports. Eventually all the Townshend Act duties, except the one on tea, were repealed.

Perhaps the most important event that showed the colonists the need for a national congress was the Boston Tea Party. On December 16, 1773, the Sons of Liberty and other Boston citizens boarded three ships carrying tea belonging to the East India Company. Disguised as Mohawk Indians, they threw 342 chests of tea into Boston Harbor. They did this to protest the tea tax and the monopoly over tea England had given the East India Company.

Years later, one young man who took part in the Boston Tea Party recalled his part in it. He wrote that:

> to prevent discovery, we agreed to wear ragged clothes and disfigure ourselves, dressed to resemble Indians as much as possible. . . . At the appointed time we met in an old building at the head of the wharf and fell in one after another, as if by accident, so as not to excite suspicion. . . . . We boarded the ship . . . Our leader told [the captain] that we were going to unload the tea...As [the chests of tea]were hauled on deck, others knocked them open with axes, and others raised them to the railing and discharged their contents overboard . . . I never worked harder in my life."[5]

Parliament Is Furious

As might be expected, Parliament did not take kindly to the news of the Boston Tea Party. When the news reached London in January 1774, one Member of Parliament declared, "The town of Boston ought to be knocked about the ears and destroyed."[6] Parliament retaliated for the Boston Tea Party by passing the Coercive Acts. Besides the Boston Port Act, the Massachusetts Government Act abolished the Massachusetts legislature. These laws, as well as other Coercive Acts, mostly affected Massachusetts, and they threatened the liberty of all Americans. The colonists would not meekly accept these laws, and Great Britain needed to know. The time had come for a national congress.

Boston residents, furious over the Townshend Acts passed by Parliament in 1767, took matters into their own hands on December 16, 1773. They destroyed 342 chests of tea by throwing them into the Boston Harbor in an act that later became known as "The Boston Tea Party."

The First Continental Congress met in Carpenters' Hall in Philadelphia. The building is still standing, and each year more than 100,000 people visit this historical site where the colonies united to free themselves from British rule.

3

Rights and Grievances

The first delegates to the First Continental Congress began arriving in Philadelphia several weeks before the official opening. Most delegations traveled together as a group. Three delegates from the South brought their wives. Other southern delegates, including George Washington, traveled with slaves.[1] All the Pennsylvania delegates lived in Philadelphia and did not have to travel.[2]

It took the four Massachusetts delegates 19 days to travel roughly 300 miles. The men, often referred to as the "New England **fanatics**," were enthusiastically greeted nearly everywhere they stopped. John Adams recorded in his diary that when the delegation reached New Haven, Connecticut, "all the Bells in Town were sett [sic] to ringing, and the People—Men, Women and Children—were crowding at the Doors and Windows as if it was to see a Coronation!"[3]

The Virginia delegates reached Philadelphia late in the afternoon of September 4. They were the last to arrive before the Congress got underway the following morning. The North Carolina delegation arrived late, when the Congress had been in session for several days.

Georgia, the newest colony, didn't send any delegates. The colony was dealing with skirmishes with Native Americans. They needed the protection of the British army and did not want to lose favor with the king.[4]

The delegates chose the East Room on the first floor of Carpenters' Hall as their meeting place. Carpenters' Hall was a new two-story brick building located near Fourth and Chestnut Streets. The second floor held Benjamin Franklin's Library Company. This was America's first lending library and the delegates were invited to use it while they were in Philadelphia.

Benjamin Franklin founded his Library Company in 1731 and it served as the first Library of Congress from the Revolutionary War until 1800. Today it is an independent research library called the Library Company of Philadelphia.

The Congress Gets Underway

Electing a president to preside over the meetings and moderate debates was the first order of business. The delegates unanimously elected Peyton Randolph, a lawyer from

The First Continental Congress opened on September 5, 1774 with a prayer offered by the Reverend Jacob Duché, the rector of Christ Church of Philadelphia. The prayer was later publicized in colonial newspapers.

Charles Thomson was appointed secretary of both the First and Second Continental Congresses. Only Thomson's name and that of John Hancock, president of the Second Congress, appeared on the first published version of the Declaration of Independence in July 1776.

Virginia. Charles Thomson, a Philadelphia teacher who was not an official delegate, was appointed secretary. His main jobs were recording the **minutes** of the congressional meetings and attending to other **clerical** duties.

Before the congress officially opened, the delegates established three rules. First, they agreed that no man would speak more than twice on the same subject without permission from the other delegates. Second, the doors to the meeting room would remain closed while discussions were underway. This way, the public would not hear what the delegates were talking about. Third, everything would be kept secret while Congress was in session. Later, after the congress adjourned, accounts of the discussions would be published in newspapers.

How Should the Votes Be Counted?

Since each colony had sent a different number of delegates, it was necessary to decide how to count the votes. New York, with eight delegates, had the largest delegation, while New Hampshire and Rhode Island each had just two. If each delegate counted as one vote, some colonies would be outvoted by others. In addition, if each delegate voted only for himself and not alongside the others from his colony, one colony might vote both for and against the same issue.

In the middle of all the quibbling, the fiery Patrick Henry, a delegate from Virginia, reminded the congress of its purpose. "The distinctions between Virginians, Pennsylvanians, New Yorkers and New Englanders, are no more," he said. "I am not a Virginian, but an American."[5]

Patrick Henry was a Virginia planter and lawyer who was known for inspiring the First Continental Congress with his passionate speeches. Because of this, Henry is often called the "Voice" of the American Revolution.

The delegates decided that "in determining questions of this Congress, each Colony or Province shall have one vote."[6] Colonies with delegates whose opinions differed from one another would either have to decide how to vote among themselves or wait for instructions from their legislatures before casting their votes.

The delegates formed committees, or small work groups. One, the Grand Committee, was put in charge of making a list of the colonies' rights and when and how England had violated them. This committee, composed of two delegates from each colony, also had to decide the best way for the colonists to receive **reparations** for these grievances. Another committee, the Committee on Parliamentary Statutes, was to list the acts of Parliament that hurt American trade and commerce. One delegate per colony took part in this committee.

The Key Question

As the congress opened, one question was on every delegate's mind. Would Massachusetts be the only colony to call for outright rebellion, or would the other colonies support her? Sympathy for Boston had been overwhelming after the Boston Port Act had closed its port. Many colonies sent food and letters of support.

For example, on September 20, 1774, John Harvey, the president of the first North Carolina Provincial Congress, sent a letter to the Massachusetts Committee of Correspondence. He wrote that "the American inhabitants of [Perquimans County, North Carolina] entertain a just sense of the sufferings of our brethren in Boston and have yet hopes that when the united determinations of the continent reaches the royal ear, they will have redress from the cruel, unjust, illegal and oppressive late acts of the British Parliament."[7]

Caleb Bull, a member of the committee of correspondence for Hartford, Connecticut, also communicated with Boston. On October 17, 1774, he wrote that the inhabitants of his town were sending the Boston neighborhood of Charlestown, "seven hundred and thirty-eight bushels of rye, and eleven bushels of corn . . . for the use and the benefit of the distressed inhabitants . . . for whose savage treatment we feel the greatest emotions of resentment."[8]

Boston had received many such letters. Helping a sister colony in a time of need was heroic and noble. But participating in outright rebellion was another matter entirely. Rebellion was considered treason in the eyes of the king, and the punishment for treason was hanging.

The Goal of the Congress

The goal of the First Continental Congress was not treason. At this point, it wasn't even independence. Rather, it had been called to give the colonies a way to protest their unfair treatment by the British government. The colonists still considered themselves loyal subjects of King George, and they truly wanted **reconciliation**. Even the "fanatics" from Massachusetts were hopeful that there would be "restoration of union & harmony between Great Britain and the Colonies, most ardently desired by all good men."[9]

Like many delegates, George Washington was not sure if he could back the Massachusetts delegates. Before leaving for Philadelphia, Washington sent a letter to his boyhood friend, Bryan Fairfax. "I shall not undertake to say where the line between Great Britain and the Colonies should be drawn, but I am clearly of opinion that one ought to be drawn; & our rights clearly ascertained,"[10] he wrote.

King George III was crowned King of Great Britain on October 25, 1760 and ruled until his death in 1820 at the age of 81. At the time of the First Continental Congress, King George saw himself as a kind father and the colonies as disobedient children. He never understood why the colonies wanted their freedom.

4

Declarations and Resolutions

"All America waited in anxious hope and expectation the decisions of a continental congress,"[1] wrote Mercy Otis Warren in her early history of the United States, published in 1805. And while America waited to see what would come from the First Continental Congress, the delegates were hard at work, pondering the best way to approach King George. Was it better to forcefully demand their rights from the King? Or should Congress take a more peaceful approach and propose a compromise? Should the colonists send representatives to Parliament? Should there be negotiations?

Joseph Galloway of Pennsylvania wanted a peaceful reconciliation with King George. Galloway created his own plan, which he called "A Plan of Union of Great Britain and the Colonies." The "Galloway Plan," as it was known in Congress, called for a new **legislative** body called the Grand Council to be formed in the colonies.

Under Galloway's plan, the Grand Council and Parliament would have to agree on any law or tax that affected the colonies. In addition, each ruling body would be able to veto the other in colonial matters. The colonists

George Galloway proposed his own Galloway Plan for easing the tensions between Great Britain and her 13 colonies. The plan was rejected by the First Continental Congress and Galloway did not attend the Second Continental Congress. He remained loyal to the crown. In 1778, he sailed to Great Britain and never returned to America.

would elect members of the Grand Council. There would also be an American president-general appointed by the king. This person would serve as the chief administrator in the colonies.

The Galloway Plan appealed to many delegates. But others felt it was unlikely that Parliament and an American

Grand Council would be able to work together for the good of the colonies. The delegates rejected the plan by a vote of six to five.

The Suffolk Resolves

While the First Continental Congress was in session, Massachusetts colonists were holding conventions throughout their colony. On September 7, 1774, a convention in Suffolk County issued the Suffolk Resolves. This proclamation declared the Massachusetts Government Act invalid. In addition, the Suffolk Resolves called for a boycott of all goods imported from Britain unless the Coercive Acts were repealed. The Suffolk Resolves also suggested that the colonies begin raising **militias**.

Paul Revere brought a copy of the Suffolk Resolves to the First Continental Congress. On September 17, 1774, the delegates unanimously approved it. For the Massachusetts delegates, that was good news. It meant the rest of the colonies would stand beside Massachusetts.

"This was one of the happiest days of my life," wrote John Adams. "This day convinced me that America will support Massachusetts or perish with her."[2]

Two Important Statements

The First Continental Congress produced two important statements. The first, the Declaration of Resolves, is sometimes called the Declaration of Rights. The Declaration listed the colonists' protests of the Coercive Acts and their grievances, and created a colonial bill of rights. Part of the Declaration of Rights reads:

> The aforesaid [delegates, on] behalf of themselves, and their constituents, do claim, demand, and insist

> on . . . their . . . rights and liberties; which cannot be legally taken from them, altered or abridged by any power whatever, without their own consent, by their representatives in their several provincial legislatures.[3]

It closes, "To these grievous acts and measures Americans cannot submit, but in hopes that their fellow subjects in Great Britain will, on a revision of them, restore us to that state in which both countries found happiness and prosperity."[4] The message of the Declaration was that the colonists would no longer obey rules made by Parliament. It would only recognize the king and deal only with him.

The second statement was the Continental Association. This called for a complete ban of all trade between Great Britain and the colonies, starting December 1, 1774. The delegates hoped that this ban would cause the repeal of the Coercive Acts. Furthermore, the Continental Association stated that if Parliament did not repeal the Coercive Acts by September, 1775, the colonies would stop exporting goods to Great Britain. Additionally, the colonists were asked to stop consuming British goods, like tea, that were already in America.

Grass-roots Participation

The delegates created a Committee of Inspection to enforce the Continental Association. Every county, city, and town would be watched to make sure British goods were not imported, exported, or consumed. Anyone found violating the Colonial Association would be considered "the enemies of American liberty; and thenceforth we respectively will break off all dealings with him or her."[5]

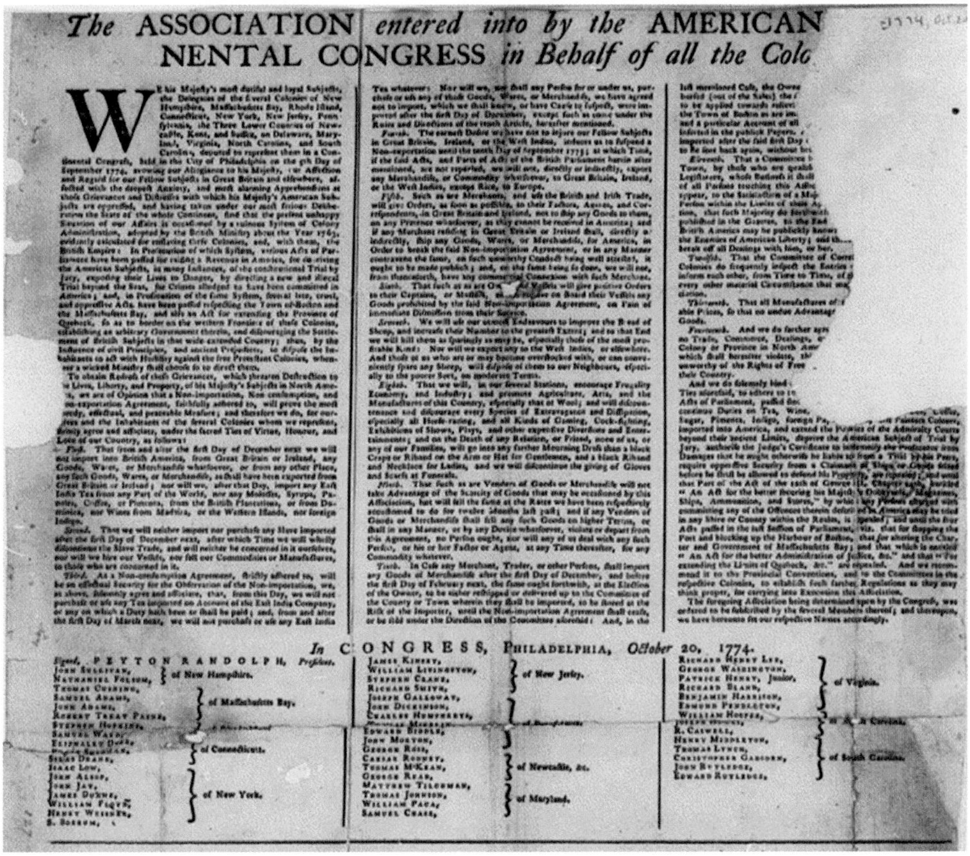
The ASSOCIATION entered into by the AMERICAN [CONTI]NENTAL CONGRESS in Behalf of all the Colo[nies]

In CONGRESS, PHILADELPHIA, October 20, 1774.

Although the purpose of the Continental Association was to use trade as a way of making Parliament repeal restrictive laws, the document opened with a statement assuring King George III that the colonists were "his Majesty's most loyal subjects."

The Continental Association was successful because it allowed the average citizen to participate in the goals of the Congress. Not every colonist could be a delegate to Congress, but every colonist could stop drinking tea imported from England. Every colonist could stop buying British cloth and start making clothes from **homespun**. Every colonist could stop buying British paper and begin making his own. Average colonists could make these sacrifices and feel they were doing their part.

A cage of starving jailed Boston citizens hangs from the Liberty Tree in this British political cartoon. The cartoon appeared in the British press after the First Continental Congress sent a petition to King George III asking him to repeal the Coercive Acts. The illustration was meant to show the colonists were weakening under the Coercive Acts, when in reality, the colonists were uniting and becoming stronger in their desire for independence.

5

Onward to Independence

The First Continental Congress drafted several additional letters. The first was "An address to the People of Great Britain." Since the delegates still saw themselves as the king's loyal subjects, they felt united with those who lived in England. The message, addressed to their "Friends and Fellow Subjects," explained the ways Parliament had hurt the colonists. The letter emphasized that the colonists did not want independence from Great Britain. They wanted only to be "as free as yourselves." If they were, the delegates wrote, they would "ever be ready to contribute all in our power to the welfare of the Empire."[1]

The delegates also wrote a letter to their fellow colonists called the "Address to the Inhabitants of the Several Anglo-American Colonies." Part of the address read, "As the situation of public affairs grows daily more and more alarming . . . it may be more satisfactory to you to be informed by us in a collective body, [rather] than in any other manner, of those sentiments that have been approved, upon a full and free discussion, by the representatives of so great a part of America."[2] The letter explained what the First Continental Congress had done for the colonists and why. The delegates represented the people. They had done what they felt was best for the people, and they wanted everyone to know this.

"A Petition of Congress to the King" was the third letter. It said that his "most faithful Subjects" were loyal to him and asked him to **intervene** with Parliament by persuading Parliament to return the colonists' rights that it had taken away. Going forward, the Congress stated, it would deal only with the king and not Parliament. The address wished "your majesty . . . every felicity through a long and glorious reign over loyal and happy subjects."[3]

An Unhappy King

King George was not happy that the colonists had held the First Continental Congress. He called it an "illegal body," and refused to read the address the Congress sent him. Unable or unwilling to understand the needs of the colonies, he continued to ignore their wishes. "The die is now cast; the colonies must either submit or triumph . . . we must not retreat,"[4] he told Lord North, the prime minister of England. He meant England would not change the way it treated the colonies. Nor could the colonies turn back after holding a congress. In the end, only one would win the struggle that was sure to come.

One Member of Parliament, Edmund Burke, believed that it was possible to make peace with the colonies. On March 22, 1775, he presented a "Speech on Concilation [sic] with the Colonies" to Parliament. "To prove that the Americans ought not to be free, we are obliged to **depreciate** the value of freedom itself,"[5] he said. His speech shows that not everyone in Parliament opposed giving the colonies their freedom.

Edmund Burke was one of a very few members of Parliament who believed Great Britain was not properly responding to the colonies' concerns. He believed it was better to show respect to the colonies instead of forcing them to follow laws that taxed them and caused hardship.

The First Continental Congress adjourned on October 26, 1774. The delegates agreed to meet again in May the following year, unless the king and Parliament addressed their grievances. While hopeful that a Second Continental Congress would not have to be called, at the same time the delegates knew that events had been put in motion that could result in all-out war. One delegate, John Dickinson, wrote to a friend, "The most peaceable Provinces, are now animated; and a Civil War is unavoidable, unless there be a quick Change of British Measures."[6]

In the spring of 1775, Parliament declared Massachusetts to be in a state of rebellion. It punished many of the other colonies for attending the First Continental Congress with additional restrictions on their commerce. Like the Coercive Acts, Parliament's newest punishment only brought the colonies closer.

The Battles of Concord and Lexington in April 1775 are considered the beginning of the Revolutionary War. The patriots claimed victory because they successfully drove the British back to Boston. The British claimed victory because they confiscated weapons at Concord.

The Revolutionary War Begins

The Second Continental Congress convened in May 1775. By that time, the gunshots at Concord and Lexington that started the Revolutionary War had been fired. On July 6, 1775, the Second Continental Congress adopted a resolution entitled "Declaration of the Causes and Necessity of Taking Up Arms." This declaration outlined the colonies' reasons for going to war with England. Almost exactly one year later, the delegates adopted the Declaration of Independence. This document, one of the most important in the history of the world, gave birth to the United States.

Americans owe a great deal to the First Continental Congress. It accomplished many things in the few short weeks it was in session. Most important, it marked the first step on the road that led to independence from Great Britain. A number of its delegates also attended the Second Continental Congress and signed the Declaration of Independence. In addition, many delegates went on to serve young America as governors, military leaders, statesmen, and justices. Two members of the First Continental Congress—George Washington and John Adams—became the first and second presidents of the United States of America.

Because of the First Continental Congress, 13 individual colonies would eventually become the United States of America.

The Second Continental Congress was called in May 1775. Unlike the First Continental Congress in which the delegates still considered themselves loyal subjects of King George III, those attending the Second Continental Congress now understood that their only option was to issue a Declaration of Independence.

APPENDIX

DELEGATES TO THE FIRST CONTINENTAL CONGRESS

MASSACHUSETTS BAY

John Adams (1735-1826) was a lawyer who served as a diplomat for the colonies during the Revolutionary War and later became the United States' first vice president and its second president.

Samuel Adams (1722-1803) was called the "Firebrand of the Revolution" for his radical ideas. He was an active promoter of colonial resistance to the King.

Thomas Cushing (1725-1788) was also a delegate to the Second Continental Congress, but was asked to leave because he opposed independence. He became lieutenant governor of Massachusetts.

Robert Treat Paine (1731-1814) was a clergyman and lawyer who later was one of the founding members of the American Academy of Arts and Sciences.

RHODE ISLAND

Stephen Hopkins (1707-1785) was a member of the Rhode Island Committee of Correspondence who began promoting independence as early as 1762 when he published a pamphlet entitled "The Rights of the Colonies Examined."

Samuel Ward (1725-1776) was a farmer who served as Rhode Island Supreme Court chief justice and governor of Rhode Island colony. He died from smallpox during the Second Continental Congress.

CONNECTICUT

Eliphalet Dyer (1721-1801) was a member of the Stamp Act Congress and a chief justice for the state of Connecticut.

Roger Sherman (1721-1793) later became a member of the committee that drafted the Declaration of Independence. He is the only member of the First Continental Congress to have also signed the Declaration of Independence, the Articles of Confederation, and the Constitution.

Silas Deane (1737-1789) was a merchant who also served as a diplomat to France during the Revolutionary War. He never returned to the United States and died under mysterious circumstances.

NEW YORK

Isaac Low (1735-1791) was president of New York's Committee of Correspondence. He later was accused of treason and emigrated to Great Britain.

John Alsop (1724-1794) was a merchant who helped keep the Continental Army provisioned. His home was captured by the British during the war.

John Jay (1745-1829) became president of the Second Continental Congress in 1778 and the first chief justice of the U.S. Supreme Court.

APPENDIX

DELEGATES TO THE FIRST CONTINENTAL CONGRESS

NEW YORK (continued)

Philip Livingston (1716-1778) was a merchant who initially opposed independence. He continued in public service until his death.

James Duane (1733-1797) was a lawyer and judge who also served as mayor of New York City.

William Floyd (1734-1821) was a wealthy landowner whose property was ransacked by the British and Loyalists during the Revolutionary War. He went on to serve in the first United States Congress.

Henry Wisner (1720-1790) helped the Continental Army by building gunpowder mills.

Simon Boerum (1724-1775) supported the radical members of the First Continental Congress and helped defeat the Galloway Plan. He took sick while attending the Second Continental Congress and died.

NEW JERSEY

James Kinsey (1731-1803) was a lawyer who became chief justice of the New Jersey Supreme Court.

William Livingston (1723-1790) became the governor of New Jersey in 1776. He also led a militia unit during the Revolutionary War.

Stephen Crane (1709-1780) opposed separation from Great Britain in the Second Continental Congress and was replaced as a delegate. His great-great-grandson Stephen Crane wrote *The Red Badge of Courage*.

Richard Smith (1735-1803) was a lawyer who practiced in Philadelphia and New Jersey. He was a member of the New Jersey Senate and also served as New Jersey state treasurer.

John de Hart (1727-1795) served on the committee that drafted the New Jersey Constitution. He resigned from the Second Continental Congress over differences about how to deal with the king.

PENNSYLVANIA

Joseph Galloway (1731-1803) became a Loyalist after the defeat of his Galloway Plan during the First Continental Congress. He settled in Great Britain.

John Dickinson (1732-1808) briefly served as a brigadier general during the Revolutionary War. He was also an author and one of the wealthiest men in the colonies.

Charles Humphrey (1714-1786) was a Quaker who voted against the Declaration of Independence and resigned from the Second Continental Congress shortly thereafter.

Thomas Mifflin (1744-1800) was a merchant and major general in the Continental Army. He was the first governor of Pennsylvania.

Edward Biddle (1738-1779) was a captain in the French and Indian War. He was a member of the committee that drafted the Declaration of Rights.

APPENDIX

DELEGATES TO THE FIRST CONTINENTAL CONGRESS

PENNSYLVANIA (continued)

John Morton (1724-1777) was a delegate to the Stamp Act Congress. He worked on the Articles of Confederation.

George Ross (1730-1779) was a lawyer and a colonel in the Continental Army. He later signed the Declaration of Independence.

DELAWARE

Caesar Rodney (1728-1784) was a member of the Stamp Act Congress and the Delaware Committee of Correspondence. He served in the Delaware Militia during the war.

Thomas McKean (1734-1817) served as governor of Pennsylvania for nine years.

George Read (1733-1789) was a lawyer who served as a state senator and the chief justice of the State of Delaware.

MARYLAND

Matthew Tilghman (1718-1790) was a plantation owner who went on to be a state senator.

Thomas Johnson (1732-1819) served as the first governor of Maryland. President Washington nominated him as Secretary of State, but he declined.

William Paca (1740-1799) later served as governor of Maryland.

Samuel Chase (1741-1811) was known in the First Continental Congress for his radical views.

Robert Goldsborough (1733-1788) was a lawyer. He resigned from the Second Continental Congress before the Declaration of Independence was signed.

VIRGINIA

Peyton Randolph (1721-1775) was, in addition to being the first president of the Continental Congress, attorney general and Speaker of the House of Burgesses in his home colony of Virginia. He died before the Declaration of Independence was signed.

Richard Henry Lee (1732-1794) also attended the Second Continental Congress, where he encouraged independence from Great Britain.

George Washington (1732-1799) went on to become the commander-in-chief of the Continental Army during the Revolutionary War and then the first president of the United States.

Patrick Henry (1736-1799) was a farmer and attorney who became the first and sixth governor of Virginia. He is especially remembered for his "Give Me Liberty or Give Me Death" speech.

Richard Bland (1710-1776) was Thomas Jefferson's cousin. He attended the Second Continental Congress but returned home before the Declaration of Independence was signed and died shortly after.

APPENDIX

DELEGATES TO THE FIRST CONTINENTAL CONGRESS

VIRGINIA (continued)

Benjamin Harrison (1726-1791) also attended the Second Continental Congress. His son, William Henry Harrison, and his great-grandson, Benjamin Harris, both became U.S. presidents.

Edmund Pendleton (1721-1803) was a farmer, lawyer, and judge. He was also a member of the Virginia Committee of Correspondence.

NORTH CAROLINA

William Hooper (1742-1790) was a physician who also attended the Second Continental Congress.

Joseph Hewes (1730-1779) was a shipping merchant who was a committee of correspondence member. He allowed the Continental Navy to use his ships during the Revolutionary War.

Richard Caswell (1729-1789) was a lawyer and surveyor who commanded a unit of minutemen during the Revolutionary War. He was the first and fifth governor of North Carolina.

SOUTH CAROLINA

Henry Middleton (1718-1784) was a farmer who was elected to be the second president of the Continental Congress.

Thomas Lynch Jr. (1749-ca. 1779) signed the Declaration of Independence, then retired. He sailed to the West Indies for health reasons, but his ship was lost at sea.

Christopher Gadsden (1724-1805) was a fierce supporter of independence. He designed the Gadsden Flag, which shows a coiled rattlesnake ready to strike and the legend "Don't Tread on Me."

John Rutledge (1739-1800) became the first governor of South Carolina and the second chief justice of the U.S. Supreme Court.

Edward Rutledge (1749-1800) was the youngest member of the First Continental Congress. He was a captain of an artillery battalion in the Revolutionary War. He became governor of South Carolina.

NEW HAMPSHIRE

Nathaniel Folsom (1726-1790) was a merchant. He became major general of the New Hampshire Militia.

John Sullivan (1740-1795) became a general in the Revolutionary War. He was involved with the ratification of the Constitution and also served as governor of New Hampshire.

CHAPTER NOTES

Chapter 1: Gentlemen Meeting Together

1. John Penn, "Report to London, 1774," quoted in John A. Neuenschwander, *The Middle Colonies and the Coming of the American Revolution* (Port Washington, NY: Kennikat Press, 1973), pp. 36-37.

2. "First Continental Congress," United States History. http://www.u-s-history.com/pages/h650.html

3. Daniel R. Goodlowe, *The birth of the republic: compiled from the national and colonial histories and historical collections, from the American archives and from memoirs, and from the journals and proceedings of the British Parliament* (Chicago: Bedford Clark, 1889), p. 179.

4. Richard Beeman, *Our Lives, Our Fortune, Our Sacred Honor* (New York: Basic Books, 2013), p. 40.

5. Ibid., pp. 41-42.

6. Ibid., pp. 57-59.

7. John Adams, *The Work of John Adams, Second President of the United States* (notes by Charles Francis Adams). (New York: Little Brown, 1856), p. 153.

Chapter 2: The Road to Philadelphia

1. "Boston Merchants' Appeals to Repeal the Sugar Act, 1764," *The Boston News-Letter and New-England Chronicle*, May 31,1764. Reprinted in "America in Class: Making the Revolution: America 1763-1791: A Primary Source Collection." http://americainclass.org/sources/makingrevolution/crisis/text2/sugaractresponse1764.pdf

2. *Pennsylvania Journal*, August 23, 1764. Quoted in *The Stamp Act Crisis: Prologue to Revolution*, Edmund S. Morgan and Helen M. Morgan (Chapel Hill, NC: University of North Carolina Press, 1953), p. 33.

3. Jedidiah Morse, *Annals of the American Revolution: Or, A Record of the Causes and Events which Produced, and Terminated in the Establishment and Independence of the American Republic . . . ; to which is Prefixed a Summary Account of the First Settlement of the Country, and Some of the Principal Indian Wars . . . ; to which is Added . . . an Appendix, Containing a Biography of the Principal Military Officers, who Were Instrumental in Achieving Our Independence.* Hartford: No publisher, 1824.

4. "The Declaration of the Rights of the Stamp Act Congress, October 19, 1765." http://www.constitution.org/bcp/dor_sac.htm

5. Francis S. Drake, ed. *Tea leaves: being a collection of letters and documents relating to the shipment of tea to the American colonies in the year 1773, by the East India tea company* (Boston: A. O. Crane, 1884), pp. 71-72.

6. Richard Beeman, *Our Lives, Our Fortune, Our Sacred Honor* (New York: Basic Books, 2013), p. 25.

Chapter 3: Rights and Grievances

1. Richard Beeman, *Our Lives, Our Fortune, Our Sacred Honor* (New York: Basic Books, 2013), p. 46.

2. Ibid.

3. John Adams, *Diary and Autobiography*. Volume 2 (Cambridge, MA: Belknap Press, 1961), p. 100.

4. Beeman, p. 39.

5. Patrick Henry: Speech to the First Continental Congress. https://www.milestonedocuments.com/documents/view/patrick-henrys-speech-to-the-first-continental-congress/text

6. Ray Raphael, *Founders: The People Who Brought You a Nation* (New York: New Press, 2009), p. 157.

7. Letter from John Harvey to the Massachusetts Committee of Correspondence, September 20, 1774. *Collections of the Massachusetts Historical Society* (Boston: Little Brown and Company, 1858), p. 85.

8. Ibid., p. 89.

9. "Resolutions of the House of Representatives of Massachusetts." http://lincoln.lib.niu.edu/cgi-bin/amarch/getdoc.pl?/var/lib/philologic/databases/amarch/.456

10. Jarad Sparks, editor. *The Writings of George Washington being his correspondence, messages, addresses, and other papers, official and private selected and published from the original manuscripts, with a life of the author* (Boston: Russel, Odiorne and Metcalf, and Hilliard, Gray, and Co., 1834), p. 398.

Chapter 4: Declarations and Resolutions

1. Mercy Otis Warren, *History of the Rise, Progress, and Termination of the American Revolution: Interspersed with Biographical, Political and Moral Observations*, Volume 1 (Boston: Manning and Loring, 1805), p. 147.

2. John Adams, *Diary and Autobiography*. Volume 2 (Cambridge, MA: Belknap Press, 1961), pp. 134-135.

3. "Declaration and Resolves of the First Continental Congress." http://www.ushistory.org/declaration/related/decres.htm

4. Ibid.

5. "The Continental Association." http://explorepahistory.com/odocument.php?docId=1-4-133

Chapter 5: Onward to Independence

1. "Address to people of Great Britain." http://www.ushistory.org/declaration/related/decres.htm#peoplegb

2. "To the Inhabitants of the Several Anglo-American Colonies." http://www.ushistory.org/declaration/related/decres.htm#oct21

3. "Petition of Congress to the King." http://www.ushistory.org/declaration/related/decres.htm#oct21

4. "American Revolution Quotations," alpha history. http://alphahistory.com/americanrevolution/american-revolution-quotations/

5. "Edmund Burke, Speech on Conciliation with the Colonies, 22 Mar. 1775." http://press-pubs.uchicago.edu/founders/documents/v1ch1s2.html

6. Paul H. Smith, *Letters of Delegates to Congress* (Washington, DC: U.S. Government Printing Office, 1976), p. 250.

FURTHER READING

Brooks, Phillip. *King George III: America's Enemy* (Wicked History). New York: Franklin Watts, 2009.

Burnett, Betty. *The Continental Congress: A Primary Source History of the Formation of America's New Government*. New York: Rosen, 2004.

Conklin, Wendy. *Early Congresses* (Primary Source Readers). Westminster, CA: Teacher Created Materials, 2004.

Freeman, Russell. *The Boston Tea Party*. New York: Holiday House, 2013.

Harness, Cheryl. *Revolutionary John Adams.* Washington, DC: National Geographic Books, 2006.

Klepeis, Alicia. *Stamp Act Congress.* Hallandale, FL: Mitchell Lane Publishers, 2018.

Santella, Andrew. *The French and Indian War.* New York: Children's Press, 2011.

Sutcliffe, Jane. *John Adams* (History Maker Bios). Minneapolis, MN: Lerner, 2006.

PRIMARY SOURCES CONSULTED

Adams, John. *The Work of John Adams, Second President of the United States* (notes by Charles Francis Adams). New York: Little Brown, 1856.

"Address to people of Great Britain." http://www.ushistory.org/declaration/related/decres.htm#peoplegb

"Boston Merchants' Appeals to Repeal the Sugar Act, 1764." *The Boston News-Letter and New-England Chronicle*, 31 May1764. Reprinted in America in Class: Making the Revolution: America 1763-1791: A Primary Source Collection. http://americainclass.org/sources/makingrevolution/crisis/text2/sugaractresponse1764.pdf

Collections of the Massachusetts Historical Society. Volume 4. Boston: Little Brown and Company, 1858.

"The Continental Association." http://explorepahistory.com/odocument.php?docId=1-4-133

"Declaration and Resolves of the First Continental Congress." http://www.ushistory.org/declaration/related/decres.htm

"The Declaration of the Rights of the Stamp Act Congress, October 19, 1765." http://www.constitution.org/bcp/dor_sac.htm

Drake, Francis S., ed. *Tea leaves: being a collection of letters and documents relating to the shipment of tea to the American colonies in the year 1773, by the East India tea company.* Boston: A. O. Crane, 1884.

"Edmund Burke, Speech on Conciliation with the Colonies, 22 Mar. 1775." http://press-pubs.uchicago.edu/founders/documents/v1ch1s2.html

Goodlowe. Daniel R. *The birth of the republic: compiled from the national and colonial histories and historical collections, from the American archives and from memoirs, and from the journals and proceedings of the British Parliament*. Chicago: Bedford Clark, 1889.

Morse, Jedidiah. *Annals of the American Revolution: Or, A Record of the Causes and Events which Produced, and Terminated in the Establishment and Independence of the American Republic . . . ; to which is Prefixed a Summary Account of the First Settlement of the Country, and Some of the Principal Indian Wars . . . ; to which is Added . . . an Appendix, Containing a Biography of the Principal Military Officers, who Were Instrumental in Achieving Our Independence.* Hartford, CT: No publisher, 1824.

PRIMARY SOURCES CONSULTED

"Patrick Henry: Speech to the First Continental Congress" https://www.milestonedocuments.com/documents/view/patrick-henrys-speech-to-the-first-continental-congress/text

Pennsylvania Journal, August 23, 1764. Quoted in *The Stamp Act Crisis: Prologue to Revolution.* Edmund S. Morgan and Helen M. Morgan. Chapel Hill, NC: University of North Carolina Press, 1953, p. 33.

"Petition of Congress to the King." http://www.ushistory.org/declaration/related/decres.htm#oct21

"Resolutions of the House of Representatives of Massachusetts." http://lincoln.lib.niu.edu/cgi-bin/amarch/getdoc.pl?/var/lib/philologic/databases/amarch/.456

Smith, Paul H. *Letters of Delegates to Congress.* Washington, DC: U.S. Government Printing Office, 1976.

Sparks, Jarad (editor). *The Writings of George Washington being his correspondence, messages, addresses, and other papers, official and private selected and published from the original manuscripts, with a life of the author.* Jared Sparks (ed.). Boston: Russel, Odiorne and Metcalf, and Hilliard, Gray, and Co., 1834.

"To the Inhabitants of the Several Anglo-American Colonies." http://www.ushistory.org/declaration/related/decres.htm#oct21

Warren, Mercy Otis. *History of the Rise, Progress, and Termination of the American Revolution: Interspersed with Biographical, Political and Moral Observations,* Volume 1. Boston: Manning and Loring, 1805.

ADDITIONAL SOURCES CONSULTED

Adams, John. *Diary and Autobiography,* Volume 2. Cambridge, MA: Belknap Press, 1961.

America in Class: Making the Revolution: America 1763-1791: A Primary Source Collection. http://americainclass.org/sources/makingrevolution/crisis/text2/sugaractresponse1764.pdf

"American History Quotes" http://alphahistory.com/americanrevolution/american-revolution-quotations/

Beeman, Richard R. *Our Lives, Our Fortunes, Our Sacred Honor.* New York: Basic Books,2013.

Copeland, Richard. *Debating the Issues in Colonial Newspapers: Primary Documents on Events of the Period.* Westport, CT: Greenwood Press, 2000.

Findling, John E. and Frank W. Thackeray, eds. *Events that Changed America in the Eighteenth Century.* Westport, CT: Greenwood Press, 1998.

"First Continental Congress." U.S. History. http://www.u-s-history.com/pages/h650.html

Greene, Jack P., editor. *Colonies to Nation, 1763-1789.* New York: McGraw-Hill, 1967.

Jaycox, Faith. *The Colonial Era: An Eyewitness History.* New York: Facts on File, 2002.

Morgan, Edmund S. and Helen M. Morgan. *The Stamp Act Crisis: Prologue to Revolution.* Chapel Hill, NC: University of North Carolina Press, 1953.

Neuenschwander, John A. *The Middle Colonies and the Coming of the American Revolution.* Port Washington, NY: Kennikat Press, 1973.

Rakove, Jack N. *The Beginnings of National Politics: The Interpretive History of the Continental Congress.* New York: Alfred Knopf, 1979.

Raphael, Ray. *Founders: The People Who Brought You a Nation.* New York: New Press, 2009.

GLOSSARY

adamant (AD-uh-muhnt)—refusal to change one's mind

agenda (uh-JEHN-duh)—plan for what will be discussed at a meeting

bankrupt (BANGK-ruhpt)—having little or no money

boycott (BOI-caht)—a ban on purchases from a particular organization as a form of protest

brigantine (BRIG-uhn-teen)—a two-masted sailing ship

clerical (KLER-uh-kuhl)—office work like organizing documents

depreciate (dih-PRIH-shee-yate)—to reduce the value of

eclectic (ih-KLEK-tik)—a mixture

economy (ih-KON-uh-mee)—having to do with money or finances

fanatic (fuh-NAA-tik)—someone who takes things to the extreme

grievance (GREE-vuhns)—a wrong that has been committed

homespun (HOHM-spuhn)—cloth made from yarn spun at home

intervene (in-tuhr-VEEN)—to step in between

legislative (LEJ-is-lay-tiv)—having to do with the making of laws

minutes (MIN-its)—the written record of a meeting

political (puh-LIT-uh-kuhl)—relating to the government or the affairs of a country

province (PRAHV-ins)—a small territory or region

reparations (rep-uh-RAY-shuns)—making amends for a wrong committed against another person

simultaneously (sy-muhl-TAY-nee-uhs-lee)—occurring at the same time as something else

smuggle (SMUGH-uhl)—bring goods into a country secretly and illegally

PHOTO CREDITS: All design elements from Thinkstock/Sharon Beck. Cover, pp. 1, 23, 37— U.S. Capitol/public domain; pp. 4, 18, 21, 36—North Wind Picture Archives/Alamy Stock Photo; p. 6—Chronicle/Alamy Stock Photo; p. 10—ClassicStock/Alamy Stock Photo; pp. 13, 31—Library of Congress; p. 15—Pictorial Press Ltd/Alamy Stock Photo; p. 17—Nathan Currier/public domain; pp. 20, 32—Photo Researchers, Inc/Alamy Stock Photo; p. 22—Joseph Wright/The U.S. Diplomacy Center exhibition page/public domain; p. 26—Johan Zoffany/The Royal Collection/Public Domain; p. 28—Thomas Emmet/public domain/New York Public Library; p. 35—Joshua Reynolds/National Portrait Gallery/public domain.

INDEX

About the Author

Marylou Morano Kjelle is a college English professor, freelance writer, and photojournalist. She has written dozens of nonfiction books for young readers, many of them about American history. She lives in New Jersey near the site of the Revolutionary War Battle of Short Hills (June 26, 1777). Based on her personal research, Marylou believes British soldiers advanced over the land on which her home stands today.